THE LITTLE BOOK OF
IRISHISMS

Know the Irish through our Words

The Little Book of Irishisms

Aimee Alexander is the pen name of bestselling
Irish author Denise Deegan.

THE LITTLE BOOK OF
IRISHISMS

Know the Irish through our Words

Written by

Aimee Alexander

Interior artwork illustrated by

Aimée Concannon

Also by Aimee Alexander

Season of Second Chances

The Accidental Life of Greg Millar

Pause to Rewind

All We Have Lost

By Denise Deegan

Through the Barricades

And By The Way

And For Your Information

And Actually

Tweet the author

@aimeealexbooks

Find out more on

www.aimeealexander.com

To my good friend, Melanie Evans,
one of the special ones.

Contents

What's In Store 9

How To Say Hello Like An Irish person 12

Ask Us How We Are…
   If You Want To Be Confused. 14

Want To Get Us Talking?. 17

What We Say If We Don't Believe You 19

Avoid These Like The Plague…. 21

Tricks To Make Your Sentences More Irish. 23

"Bockety" And Other Uniquely Irish Words 28

"Give It A Lash" And (Many) Other Expressions . . . 42

Words We Have Nicked And Made Our Own 69

The Uniquely Irish Use of "Grand". 84

Ask Us To Do Something Unreasonable … 87

A Few Auld Insults While We're At It 88

We Might Occasionally Compliment You. 95

"Hurling" And Other Confusing Irish Nouns.......97

Why Say "It's Raining" When You Can Say… 101

What We Call Our Mothers 103

Our Many Words For "Drunk"....................104

How Not To Win Friends.........................106

Irish Obsessions................................107

Irish Names And How To Pronounce Them....... 111

    Girls' Names 111

    Boys' Names.................................122

Impress With Some Irish Language Words 132

A Bit Of An Auld Story...........................139

Glossary....................................151

Acknowledgements 163

About The Author & Illustrator...................166

What's In Store

When travelling outside Ireland, I'm often met with a sudden blank look when chatting to other English speakers. I'll stop, realising that I've just said something that only Irish people understand. Something like, "Gimmie that yoke." They'll look at me, wondering, *What yolk? What actual egg?* At which point, I'll have to explain that when Irish people use the word "yoke" out of context, we just mean "thing." A reminder that we're speaking two very different versions of the same language.

The Little Book of Irishisms is for anyone who wants to understand Irish people – an ambitious goal but, as we say, God loves a trier. It's also for people who want to sound Irish even just for St Patrick's Day. Also ambitious. But God still loves a trier.

In this little book, you'll learn handy tricks like putting the word "fierce" in front of any noun instantly Irishifies it e.g. "He's a fierce eejit (eejit = idiot)." For maximum Irishness, add "altogether" and you're away in a hack, so to speak. "He's a fierce eejit, altogether." See? Already some classics and we're only at the Introduction.

Sometimes, Irishness comes from a unique, standalone word that is only used in Ireland e.g. "banjaxed" (meaning broken beyond repair). Sometimes the Irish flavour is achieved by how a word is used in a sentence. "You're grand," can mean "No, thanks," or "Don't worry," depending on the context. Read on; it'll all become clear.

The Little Book of Irishisms looks at single words, (words that are either uniquely Irish or that say something about what it means to be Irish), outlining their meaning, pronunciation and how they are used in a sentence. It introduces expressions that are particularly Irish. Also insults. We have many words for rain for obvious – and depressing – reasons. By popular request, I have included common Irish names and how to pronounce them. Call it a public service. Crucially – you'll discover the things that people think we say but we never actually do. For example, "May the road rise with you," is something that's only said in the Irish language, never in English. I wrap up by putting many of the words and expressions you've learned into practice in a short story. Fun to write, it has to be said. If at any point you're stuck, there's a glossary at the end.

Ready? **Let's get cracking...** So to speak.

How To Say Hello Like An Irish Person

So you touch-down in Ireland and want your "Hello!" to sound Irish but not like you're trying? You can't go wrong with: "How's it going?"

You'll also hear:

- How're you going?
- Craic? (Pronounced: crack. Meaning: news)
- What's the craic?
- How's the form?
- How's it hanging?
- How're things?
- How's things?

- Howya?
- Howrya?
- Alright?
- Well?
- How's she cutting? (Rural expression)
- How're you getting on?

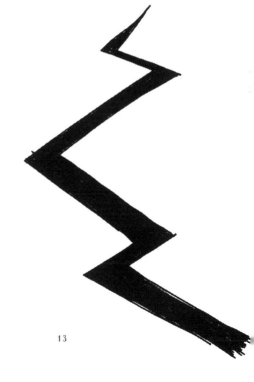

ASK US HOW we Are...

If You Want To Be Confused

When asked how we are, we Irish are not known for hyperbole. We could be feeling better or worse than our words indicate. You'll hear:

Could be better.
Bad. Possibly very bad.

Ah, sure, you know yourself.
Don't want to talk about it.

Fair to middling.
Bad. A favourite of my granny's.

Pulling the divil by the tail.
Struggling.

Not too bad.
Usually said in a positive tone to indicate that we're actually fine.

Grand / Yera, grand.
Just okay.

Fine.
Okay.

Fine and dandy.
Good.

Grand altogether / Grand out.
Actually, good. Maybe even great, depending on who's talking.

Great!
No hidden meaning here.

Mighty!
Great!

On the pig's back!
Fantastic. Derived from the Irish expression: "ar mhuin na muice" on the pig's back.

Once we say how we are, we usually flip the question back to you.

Want To Get Us Talking?

We're a pretty chatty race. If you want to get us talking – and fit right in, at the same time – just ask: **"Any craic?"** or **"What's the craic?"** Meaning "Any news?" You might even impress us that you know "craic." I say, might.

We love a bit of news / scandal. And we'll ask you for it in any number of ways...

- Any craic? / What's the craic? / Craic?
- What's the story?
- Story?
- Story, Rory? (Regardless of your name)
- Story, bud?

- What's up?
- What's the suss?
- Any scandal?
- Any sca?
- Any goss?

What We Say If We Don't Believe You

Mild surprise:

- That's gas!
- Gas!
- You're a gas ticket!
- Go away!
- Go 'way outta that!
- Go on outta that!
- Get up outta that!
- Get away!
- Stop the lights!
- Well, that beats Banagher!
- Be the hokey! (rural expression)

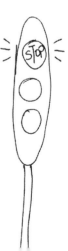

When we think you're flat-out pulling our leg:

- Come off it!
- Get off the stage!
- Get up the yard!
- You're having me on!
- That's Blarney! (less common)
- That's malarkey!

When you go too far, we're not not afraid of expletives:

- You're full of shite!
- You're talking shite!
- That's pure shite!
- That's bollix / Bollix!

Avoid These Like The Plague...

Best to avoid these unless you *want* to sound like a non-Irish person trying to sound Irish:

May the road rise with you / to meet you.
This is only ever said in the Irish language to wish you luck. We would never say it in English.

Top of the morning to you.
Only used by leprechauns.

Begorrah!
Only heard in old Hollywood movies of Ireland. And let's keep it that way.

I speak Gaelic.

We call the Irish language "Irish" not Gaelic.

Éire

Éire is the Irish word for Ireland, used when speaking Irish, not English.

St. Paddy's Day / St. Patty's Day

It's either Paddy's Day or St. Patrick's Day.

Soft day, thank God.

Not a complete mortaller (mortal sin). It *is* said, often sarcastically. But, as it is one of those go-to phrases that non-Irish people use to sound Irish, it's a bit of a clanger.

Our name for this kind of speak: **Oirish**. We do not react well.

Tricks To Make
Your Sentences More Irish

Try these tricks if you want to make your sentences sound more Irish:

- Use "fierce" instead of very e.g. "He's fierce intelligent."

- Turn a sentence into a question e.g. "Sure, where would you be?" This particular one means: "Could you be anywhere better than this?"

- For emphasis, add "altogether" after a noun at the end of a sentence e.g. "Isn't he a fierce eejit, altogether?"

- Add "at all, at all," to the end of a negative sentence e.g. "I'm not venturing out in that rain at all, at all." Again, emphasis.

- Repeat short sentences connecting them with "so" e.g. "I am so I am." "I did so I did." Emphasis is strong with us.

- Make your verbs ongoing e.g. "What would you be wanting?" "I'm going to go." "I'm going to have to do that again." "Don't be listening to him."

- Precede a sentence with: "God." "Jaysus." "Sure." "Ah, sure, look." "Yera." "Here." e.g. "Here, give me that yoke (thing)."

- If you're comfortable with expletives, choose Irish ones e.g. "Feck." "Shite." "Gobshite."

- Use "me" instead of "my" e.g. "Aw, me head."

- Use "ye" instead of you plural.

- Put "away" after an ongoing verb e.g. "I was chatting away with Mary." We do this to emphasize that it was going on for a while.

- Use "after" in the past tense e.g. use "I'm after doing," instead of "I have done."

- Instead of, "I've just done that," go for, "I'm only after doing that."

- Some people put "do be" in front of a verb: "I do be eating."

- Say "Come here," or "Come here to me" or "Come here till I tell you," or "C'mere I want ya," before imparting information. It's an instruction to lean in.

- Instead of "I'm not," say "I amn't."

- Instead of "It is," use "'Tis".

- End a sentence with "all the same." e.g. "Isn't it grand weather, all the same?"

- End a sentence with "like" e.g. "You know, like." In fact, you can liberally sprinkle your sentences with "like," especially if you're young.

- End a sentence with "boy" or "girl" if you're trying to sound like you're from Cork. You could also use "boyo" or less commonly "bucko" instead of "boy."

- Add "now" to the end of a sentence. "Here she is, now." "Don't be doing that, now."

- Add "so" to the end of a sentence. "I will, so."

- Replace "really" with: "only," "right," "bleeding," or "dead" e.g. "He's only gorgeous." "He's dead sexy." "He's a right eejit." "Did you put the bleeding cat out?" You can drop the "g" in "bleeding" if you want to go all out.

- Ask, "You know what I mean?" after a statement you've made.

- "In fairness…" or "In all fairness…" is commonly used at the start – or end – of a sentence to argue the case for something.

- To argue the case for a person, you might say, "To give him his due…"

"Bockety" And Other Uniquely Irish Words

We use some great words when speaking our version of English (Hiberno-English). Many come from the Irish language:

Aul / Auld *Adjective*

PRONOUNCED Owl / Owl'd

MEANING Old

SENTENCE

1. "Have you an auld smile, there, for your grandad?"

2. "You're an auld pet. You're an auld star."

Banjaxed (Adjective, Verb)

MEANING

1. Broken beyond repair
2. Exhausted / shattered (when referring to a person)

SENTENCE

1. "Well, you've just gone and banjaxed that now."
2. "I'm banjaxed."

COMMENT This fabulous word is dying out. Start using it today!

Banjoed *Adjective*

MEANING

1. Wrecked
2. Hungover

SENTENCE "I'm banjoed after the sesh last night."

(sesh = session)

COMMENT Slang

Begrudgery *Noun*

MEANING Resenting someone their success

SENTENCE

1. "None of that begrudgery, now."
2. "Will you stop your begrudgery."

COMMENT

1. A particularly Irish trait. We wouldn't want anyone getting a "swelled head" or "too big for their boots."
2. Equally, we would *never* want to come across as sycophantic.
3. A begrudging person is a "Begrudger" e.g. "Feck the begrudgers!"

Blaggard *Noun*

MEANING Scoundrel

SENTENCE

1. "Get that blaggard out of here."
2. "You auld blaggard."

COMMENT

1. Like many of our insults, it can also be a term of affection, depending on the tone.
2. Also used in Britain. Thought to have originated in Northern Ireland.

Bockety *Adjective*

MEANING Wobbly, rickety, unsteady

SENTENCE

1. "No wonder that table's bockety. Sure, isn't one leg shorter?"
2. "Don't sit on that. It's bockety."

COMMENT "Bockety" is derived from the Irish word "bacach" which means lame.

Codding *Verb*

MEANING

1. Tricking, fooling, misleading
2. Joking

SENTENCE

1. "Don't be codding me."
2. "Is it codding me you are?"
3. "I'm only codding."

Codology *Noun*

MEANING The art of bluffing

SENTENCE "Go away with your codology."

COMMENT "Codology!" on its own means, "You're talking rubbish!"

Craic *Noun*

PRONOUNCED Crack

MEANING

1. Fun
2. News

SENTENCES

1. "You're no craic." (You're no fun.)
2. "That was gas craic." (That was great fun.)
3. "Any craic?" (Any news?)
4. "What's the craic?" (What's up? What's the story?)

COMMENT

1. Very commonly used.
2. No relationship to drugs.
3. "Having the craic" is a very Irish aspiration.
4. To impress, ask, "Aon craic?" instead of, "Any craic?" ("Aon" is Irish for "any." Pronounced: "ain")
5. One answer to "Any craic?" is "Divil a bit!" (i.e. None.)

Culchie *Noun*

PRONOUNCED CUL-she

MEANING A rural person

SENTENCE "That place'll be full of culchies."

COMMENT A pejorative term used by Dubliners. Well, some Dubliners.

ALTERNATIVE

1. "Bogger." Someone from the bogs. Equally pejorative.
2. Slang

Dote *Noun*

MEANING Sweetie / Lovely person

SENTENCE

1. "Ah, you're an aul dote."
2. "Isn't Una the biggest dote?"

COMMENT Commonly used. A warm and genuine compliment.

Feck (Expletive)

MEANING The word we came up with to avoid using the other "F" word – which we also use – quite a bit actually.

SENTENCE "Ah, feck that anyway."

COMMENT

1. Slang. Considered harmless.
2. Ubiquitous.
3. Can also be used as a verb e.g. "What did you have to go and feck that out the window for?"
4. Can also be used as an adjective e.g. "You fecking eejit you."
5. As I say, ubiquitous.

Feoster *Verb*

MEANING To fuss or bustle around in an agitated away.

SENTENCE "She's foostering around in there, looking for her keys."

Galore *Adjective*

MEANING Lots of, plentiful

SENTENCE "I've got spuds galore."

COMMENT Origin of the word: from the Irish "go leor" meaning plenty.

Gurrier *Noun*

MEANING Thug

SENTENCE "That Pat O'Driscoll is a right gurrier."

COMMENT Origin of the word: thought to come from gur cake, a pastry historically associated with street urchins.

Holy Show *Noun*

MEANING An embarrassment

SENTENCE

1. "You're a holy show."
2. "You're making a holy show of yourself."

COMMENT This term is making a comeback.

Jackeen *Noun*

MEANING Someone from Dublin

SENTENCE "What would you expect from a Jackeen?"

COMMENT Pejorative term used by people from outside Dublin.

Mé Féiner *Noun*

PRONOUNCED May-FAY-ner

MEANING A selfish, self-obsessed person

SENTENCE "They're a shower of mé féiners."

COMMENT

1. One of the worst things you could be in Ireland.
2. We especially frown upon those who don't "stand their round" in a pub.
3. Comes from the Irish word, "mé féin," which means "myself."

Morto *Adjective*

MEANING Short for "mortified"

SENTENCE

1. "I was morto."
2. "Wouldn't you be morto?"

COMMENT More common in Dublin.

Nixer *Noun*

MEANING A job on the side that you don't declare for tax purposes.

SENTENCE

1. "It's a bit of a nixer."
2. "How about an auld nixer?"

COMMENT

3. Not necessarily frowned upon.
4. Slang

Pass-remarkable *Adjective*

MEANING Verbally judgmental, excessively critical

SENTENCE "He's fierce pass-remarkable."

Quare *Adjective*

MEANING Queer, odd, strange

SENTENCE "Quare weather we're having."

Ructions *Noun*

MEANING Uproar, quarrelsome outbreak, noisy disturbance

SENTENCE "Well, that's just caused ructions, now!"

COMMENT Origin of the word: Ireland's 1798 rebellion.

Segotia

PRONOUNCED Seg-O-sha

MEANING Pal

SENTENCE "Ah, me auld segotia!"

COMMENT Term of endearment

ALTERNATIVE "Me auld flower."

Shite *Noun*

PRONOUNCED SHYte

MEANING Shit (which we also say)

SENTENCE

1. "Ah, shite."
2. "I will in me shite." (I won't.)

COMMENT

1. Very common. We use our expletives liberally, here.
2. A "dry shite" is a bore, which is a very serious offence in Ireland.

Smithereens

MEANING In tiny pieces

SENTENCE "He smashed the glass to smithereens."

COMMENT Comes from the Irish "smidiríní" meaning little bits.

Spud *Noun*

MEANING Potato

SENTENCE "Eat your spuds."

COMMENT Nickname for people named Murphy.

Wojus *Adjective*

MEANING Bad, terrible, woeful

SENTENCE "God, isn't that a wojus jumper on yer man?"

COMMENT Slang

Yera (Expression)

MEANING Often at the start of a sentence for no particular reason.

SENTENCE "Yera, I'll give it a try."

COMMENT A bit like, "sure".

"Give It A Lash"

And (Many) Other Expressions

In no particular order, here are some common Irish expressions you might like to try:

What are you at? / What are you up to?
What are you doing?

Dolled up
Dressed up e.g. "You're all dolled up."

Raring to go
Dying to get going

You have it on arseways.
You're wearing it wrong e.g. back-to-front or inside out.

Hold tight / Hold on / Hang on / Hold your whist / Hold your horses.
Wait.

That hasn't made a blind bit of difference.
That hasn't made the slightest difference.

I'm off out.
I'm going out (Usually socially).

I'm going for a few scoops.
I'm going for a few drinks.

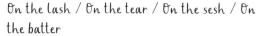

On the lash / On the tear / On the sesh / On the batter
Out on the town. Drinking.

A feed of pints / a rake of pints
A load of pints

Sound / Coola Boola / Nice one!
Cool!

Nifty!
Great! Handy! Useful! Cool!

The place was heaving / mobbed / packed / jammers.
The place was crowded.

Shooting the breeze
Chatting

Losing the head
Losing your temper

I'm broke / I'm skint.
I've no money.

He's putting on the poor-mouth.

He's pretending to have no money. Comes from the Irish "an béal bocht" (the poor mouth).

Chancing your arm / Winging it / Trying it on

The very Irish occupation of trying something in the hope that it will work.

That's malarkey!

That's rubbish!

Stand your round.

Buy the drinks when it's your turn.

Mortaller

Mortal sin. (To the Irish, not standing your round is a mortaller).

You're away in a hack.

You're flying. It'll all be easy, from now on.

Giving it socks
Being enthusiastic about something e.g. giving it socks on the dance floor.

Hup ya boy ya / Go on, ya good thing / G'wan, ya boy ya!
Go for it!

I was bricking it / I was planking it.
I was really nervous.

I was up to ninety.
I was hectic.

Give it a go / Give it a lash.
Try it. (A very common sentiment).

G'wan so / G'wan sure.
Alright, go ahead. (If someone asks if they should "Give it a go").

You might as well / You may as well.
Why not? (The general attitude in Ireland).

Fair enough.
Okay.

Fair dues to you / Fair dues / Fair play / Fair fecks / Fair / Good on you / Good man!
Good for you / Go you!

Scenes!
Good times!

Yup the sesh!
Yaay!

'Mon, we go again.
Come on, let's go on another date. (Youth speak).

He's acting the maggot / He's feckacting / Jigacting / Trickacting / Codacting.
He's messing about. He's being an idiot.

He's going baloobas.
He's going crazy altogether. Could be after drink.

The cut of him / The state o' him / The state o' yer man / The head on him / The hack of him.
He looks terrible.

He's all over the shop.
He's all over the place.

Don't make a bollix out of yourself.
Don't be an idiot.

Don't come crying to me if... / Don't come running to me if you break your leg.
If you do that, expect the worst. Typical warnings from traditional Irish mammies.

Janey / Janey Mac / Janey Mackers!
My goodness!

The gob on him.
The mouth on him. He doesn't stop talking.

Putting something on the long finger
Procrastinating. Comes from the Irish: "Ar an mhéar fhada." (Pronounced: Er on VARE fada)

Taking the piss out of someone / slagging
Mildly mocking them e.g. "Are you taking the piss?" means "Are you joking?" (Slang)

Taking you for a ride / Pulling the wool over your eyes
Treating you like a fool

Don't push it / Don't push your luck.
Don't overstep.

He'll get his comeuppance.
Karma will get him.

Go easy on him.
Give him a break.

Go easy / Take it handy.
Take it easy.

Only messing! / Only codding!
Only joking! What you say after you've been, "Taking the piss."

I'm knackered / I'm shagged / I'm wrecked.
I'm exhausted.

I'm going to head / I'm going to head off / I'm going to head on.
I'm leaving. (No one in Ireland leaves without announcing it, even if just going to the bathroom. We feel that we have to tell everyone in case they'd miss us.)

I'm going for a slash / leak.
I'm going for a pee.

Breaking the seal
Going for a pee for the first time while out drinking. After that, you'll be dashing to the loo every five minutes. Or so they say.

I'm doing a runner.
I'm making a quick exit (often without paying).

Leg it!
Run!

On your bike!
Get lost!

Gas / Gas one!
That's funny!

You're a gas ticket.
You're hilarious.

You're mad, Ted.
You're mad but in a great way. It's a line from a quirky and hugely popular comedy series called *Father Ted* (recommended, try YouTube). Irish people will be very impressed if you use this.

Is it yourself? / Would you look who it is? / 'Tis yourself!
Is that you? (If you're surprised to see someone.)

You scared the bejaysus out of me / You frightened the life out of me / You scared the shite out of me / You put the heart across me.
You gave me a huge fright.

I was away with the fairies.
I was miles away. My thoughts were elsewhere.

Thrilled skinny
Delighted

Out of his tree
Crazy. Drunk. High. You can also
be "bored out of your tree."

Sure look it / Sure look, sure listen.
What to say when you don't know
what to say. (Very commonly used.)

Ah, here!
Expression when you're not happy
with something.

Be grand!
It'll be fine!

No Bother.
You're welcome.

She's shot up.
She has gotten really tall.

There isn't a pick on her.
She's really thin.

A skinny malink
A really thin person.

She has beef to the heel.
She's chubby, especially around the ankles.
Rural saying. Comes from the expression: "Beef
to the heel like a Mullingar heifer" i.e. a cow
from Mullingar.

He's the spit of / the image of / the spitting image of...
He looks exactly like...

Bog standard
Perfectly ordinary

He has a face on him like a badly smacked arse.
He has a red and ugly face.

He's a ride / He's a fine thing / He's mint / He's some lash.

He's a good-looking guy.

He's a flah.

Same as he's a ride – but in Cork.

Doing a line with

Going out with. Expression used by the traditional Irish mammy.

I ate the head off him / I gave out to him / I gave out stink to him / I tore strips off him / I ripped into him / I lost the head with him.

I told him off. Aggressively.

Effin' and blindin'

Cursing

In floods

In tears

THE TIMES
FLOOD WARNING
CHICKEN FILLET ROLL PRICE HIKE.
POPULATION EXPECTED TO BE IN FLOODS.

He's the business / the bizz.
He's great.

He's all business / all bizz.
He's actively engaged in what he's doing.

He's not at the races / He hasn't a hope.
He's not up to it.

You've done us proud.
You've made us proud.

I'm up the duff.
I'm pregnant.

Snapper
Baby (Dublin expression)

Don't look a gift-horse in the mouth.
Be grateful.

Like hen's teeth
Rare

The curse of seven snotty orphans on you.
Curse on you.

Keep sketch.
Keep a lookout.

He made a bags of it / He made a balls of it /
He made a dog's dinner out of it / He made a
hames of it.
He made a mess of it.

Haven't seen her in donkey's years.
Haven't seen her in ages.

What's she up to?
What's she doing?

You wouldn't know what she'd be up to.
You'd never know what she's doing.

Having a whale of a time
Having a great time

What is he like?
Drawing attention to someone e.g. because of how they are acting or how they look.

That's class / Class / Mighty / Deadly / Savage!
That's great!

Where would you be?
Could you be anywhere better than this? Often said when the sun shines, which it so infrequently does, here. The sentiment would be: There's no better place than Ireland when the sun shines.

The sun was splitting the stones.
The sun was really hot. A rare occurrence.

You'd want to be up early / You can't pull the wool over his eyes / He's hard to get one over on.

You can't outsmart him.

I'm hitting the scratcher.

I'm going to bed.

In rag order

In a bad way. Could mean sick or hungover.

He has a bad dose.

He's really sick. e.g. He has a bad dose of flu.

There's a dose going around.

Everyone's getting the same illness e.g. flu.

I'm in the horrors.

I'm hungover.

Aw, sickener!

I feel your pain.

That's cat.
That's awful.

You'll be better before you're twice married.
What to tell kids when they hurt themselves.
It'll soon be over.

Your man / Your woman / Yer man / Yer woman / Your one / Yer one / Yer wan
That guy / Him / Her (Very commonly used.)
e.g. "Here, tell yer man he can't go in there."

Your only man
The best thing / person for the job. (e.g.
"A cup of tea is your only man.")

The missus
The wife

Missus
Term of endearment used between
female friends e.g. Hiya, missus.

I didn't come down in the last shower /
No flies on me.

Can't fool me.

Up to ninety

Very busy. Hectic.

Still an' all.

Nonetheless. Even so.

Jesus, Mary and Joseph / Jesus, Mary and
sweet Saint Joseph / Sweet God / Holy Jesus /
Sweet Jesus / Sweet Baby Jesus / Jesus Iscariot
/ Jaysus / Mother of God! / Holy Mother of God!

Exclamations of shock.

He's on the doss / He's dossing / He's slacking off
/ He's skiving off.

He's avoiding work.

It's a doss.
It's easy.

She's mitching.
She's skipping school.

Haven't you the life of Reilly?
Haven't you a great life?

Don't be half-arsed about it.
Try harder.

She's giving out about something.
She's complaining about something.

She's giving out to him.
She's telling him off.

Were you born in a field?
Close the door! (We're a nation obsessed with keeping doors closed.)

Plug out the TV.
Un-plug the TV.

Do the washing.
Do the laundry.

I'm going to get the messages.
I'm going grocery shopping.

Wet the tea.
Make a pot of tea (by wetting the leaves or bags with boiling water).

The trek of that / It's a trek / Trek!
It's too much like work.

You pup!
You brat! You monkey! (Usually an adult speaking to a child.)

I will in a minute / Give me a minute.
A stalling trick, said in the hope that the person
who made the request will forget about it.

She'd run rings around you.
She'd outsmart you (by a longshot).

Thanks a million / Thanks a mill.
Huge thanks. Very commonly used. Sometimes
sarcastically.

Give over / Would you give over / Dry up!
Oh, stop talking. (Milder than "Shut up" but with
the same level of irritation.)

What are you on about?

What are you talking about? (Usually said impatiently.)

What are you gawking at?

What are you staring at?

What are you on?

Are you high? Are you crazy? (Often a reply to a ridiculous statement.)

You're off your rocker / You're off your trolley / You're mad / You looper / You nutter / You mentaller / You headcase!

You're out of your mind. (Often considered a good thing e.g. "You looper," often means: "You're hilarious.")

I need to get my ass in gear.

I need to get it together. (Often a deadline.)

Piss off / Shag off / Buzz off / Flip off / Feck off!
Get lost!

Pissed off
Annoyed / fed up e.g. "I'm pissed off." Or "He pissed me off."

ALSO MEANS took off / vamoosed e.g. "He pissed off out of here a few minutes ago."

Feck sake / Sake!
Harmless expletive when something annoys you.

To get on the wrong side of someone / Put someone's back up
To irritate / annoy someone.

For the day that's in it
For the occasion (e.g. "Ah, sure, I might as well dress up for the day that's in it.)

How're you fixed?
Does it suit you (e.g. to go somewhere or do something)?

Well wear.
Wear it well. (Said to someone who is wearing something new.)

In the nip / Starkers
Naked

Excira and Delira
Excited and delighted. (Dublin expression)

It's the best thing since sliced bread / since the sliced pan.
It's great.

We're flying / We're laughing / We're sucking diesel / We're playing a blinder!
We're doing great. Things are working out for us.

Keep your hair on / Keep your wig on / Calm your jets / Cool down / Don't get your knickers in a twist.

Take it easy. Calm down.

I'm not pushed / I couldn't be bothered / I couldn't be arsed.

I don't feel like it.

It galls me.

It makes me really angry.

You have some gall / The gall of you!

You have some cheek / The cheek of you!

Bless!

Aw!

God bless.

Can be said instead of "Goodbye" or after it.

Words We Have Nicked
And Made Our Own

Welcome to words that originated elsewhere that we either use a lot or in a unique context:

Bold *Noun*

PRONOUNCED Bold. Also: "Bowld"

MEANING Naughty

SENTENCE

1. "Now, that's just bold."
2. "Don't be bold."

IRISH SAYING "You're as bold as brass."

COMMENT In Ireland, like everywhere else, we can "boldly go." But our main use of "bold" is "naughty." Very commonly used.

Bum *Verb*

MEANING Borrow

SENTENCE "Can I bum a cigarette?"

COMMENT

1. We don't use "bum" to refer to a homeless person.
2. As a noun, we use it to mean "rear end."

Cop On (Noun & Verb)

MEANING Common sense

SENTENCE

1. "You'd think he'd have some cop on."
2. "Cop on!" or "Cop yourself on!" or "Cop on to yourself!" (Have sense!)

COMMENT Commonly used.

Gallivanting *Verb*

MEANING Wandering about having fun

SENTENCE "She's off out gallivanting again."

COMMENT Irish mammies are not impressed with gallivanting.

Gammy *Adjective*

MEANING Not working properly

SENTENCE "I have a gammy leg."

COMMENT Slang

Gas (Noun & Adjective)

MEANING

1. Funny
2. Incredible

SENTENCE

1. "That's gas." Or just: "Gas!"
2. "You're gas craic." (You're great fun / You're hilarious.)

COMMENT Very commonly used.

Gouger *Noun*

MEANING Thug, swindler

SENTENCE "He's nothing but a gouger."

COMMENT Never a good thing.

Greens *Noun*

MEANING Green vegetables

SENTENCE "Eat your greens." A common request by Irish mammies.

Gurrier *Noun*

MEANING Thug, troublemaker

SENTENCE "See that gurrier? Keep well away."

Lash (Noun, Verb)

MEANING

1. Good-looking guy *Noun*
2. Drink excessively *Verb*
3. Rain heavily *Verb*
4. Try *Verb*

SENTENCES

1. "Isn't Brian O'Donnell a fierce lash?" (good-looking guy)
2. "I'm going on the lash." (I'm going out drinking.)
3. "It's lashing again." (It's raining.)
4. "Give it a lash." (Give it a try.)

COMMENT Slang

Jammy *Adjective*

MEANING Lucky

SENTENCE "You jammy bastard, you."

COMMENT There is a note of envy in the word.

Jumper *Noun*

MEANING Pullover, sweater

SENTENCE "Where's me jumper?"

COMMENT In Ireland, we would never call a person a jumper.

Kibosh *Noun*

PRONOUNCED KYE-bosh

MEANING To put the kibosh on something means to decisively end it.

SENTENCE

1. "Well, that's put the kibosh on your chances of getting into college."
2. Not uncommon for Irish parents to predict doom.

Kip *Noun*

MEANING

1. A sleep
2. A dive, a dump
3. A mess

SENTENCE

1. "I'm going for a kip." (sleep)
2. "I've never seen such a kip." (dive)
3. "Your bedroom is a complete kip." (mess)

COMMENT Slang

Lads *Noun*

MEANING Guys, pals, mates

SENTENCE

1. "Here, lads, what are ye at?"
2. "I'm off out with the lads."
3. "You think you're a real lad now, don't ya?"
4. "Aw, lads!" Expression of disappointment – often with no actual lads present.

COMMENT Very commonly used

Mouldy *Adjective*

PRONOUNCED MOWL-dy

MEANING

1. Drunk
2. Disgusting
3. Filthy

SENTENCE

1. "He was mouldy last night."
2. "Get that mouldy jumper off you."

COMMENT Just one of the many words for drunk in Ireland. More later.

Notions *Noun*

MEANING Delusions of grandeur

SENTENCE

1. "Don't be giving him notions."
2. "The notions on him!"
3. "Where did he get the notions?"
4. Or just: "Notions!"

COMMENT Possibly the worst thing you could have in Ireland. There's a perception that people with notions should be "taken down a peg or two."

Pass out *Verb*

MEANING To overtake a car

SENTENCE "Put on your indicator if you're going to pass out."

COMMENT More commonly used than "overtake."

Press *Noun*

MEANING Cupboard / Closet

SENTENCE "It's in the press."

COMMENT More commonly used than cupboard.

Pull *Verb*

MEANING Kiss, get lucky

SENTENCE "I pulled last night."

COMMENT Slang

Pure *Adjective*

MEANING Really / Typically

SENTENCE

1. "That's pure Irish."
2. "That's pure you."
3. "That's pure shite."

MEANING I don't believe you.

COMMENT There was an Irish TV drama called "Pure Mule," an expression that means either "brilliant" or "absolutely terrible" depending on the intonation.

Rig-out *Noun*

MEANING Outfit

SENTENCE "Who let her out in that rig-out?"

Scarlet *Adjective*

PRONOUNCED SCAR-let (In some parts of Dublin the 't' is not pronounced).

MEANING Really embarrassed

SENTENCE

1. "I was scarlet for ya."
2. "Scarlet for his ma for having him."

COMMENT Slang

Scaldy *Adjective*

PRONOUNCED SCAWL-dee

MEANING

1. Yuck / Disgusting / Gone off
2. Mean / Selfish
3. Rough / Thuggish

SENTENCE

1. "That cheese was scaldy."
2. "Scaldy bastard."

COMMENT Slang

Shift *Verb*

MEANING Kiss passionately, make out

SENTENCE

1. "Did you shift him last night?"
2. "Did you see the lad she shifted last night?"
3. "I heard you got the shift."

COMMENT Slang

Shower *Noun*

MEANING Group, bunch

SENTENCE "You're nothing but a shower of wasters."

COMMENT Mild insult. Slang.

Slag *Verb*

MEANING Mildly mock, make fun of

SENTENCE "Sure, I'm only slagging you."

COMMENT

1. You couldn't survive here if you weren't able for a slagging; it's that common.
2. "Slag" as a noun is an insult meaning someone promiscuous. (Slang)

Sound *Adjective*

MEANING

1. Good
2. A good guy
3. Reliable
4. Cool

SENTENCE

1. "He's sound as a pound."
2. "Sound!" on its own means "Cool!"
3. "Sound, out!" means "Great!"

COMMENT

1. Very commonly used.
2. Referring to someone as sound is a real compliment.

Spondoolicks *Noun*

MEANING Money

SENTENCE "He's not short of the auld spondoolicks."

COMMENT Slang. Similar to "lolly."

Sure (Expression)

PRONOUNCED Shur

MEANING Often at the start of a sentence, meaning nothing in particular.

SENTENCE

1. "Sure, what would I be wanting with an iPhone?"
2. "Sure, look it."
3. "Sure look. Sure listen."

COMMENT

1. "Sure, look it," is what we say when we don't know what to say. Loosely translated as: "That's life." The same goes for "Sure look. Sure listen."
2. Very commonly used.

Thick *Adjective*

PRONOUNCED Thick (or "tick" by some)

MEANING Stupid

SENTENCE

1. "Are you thick, or what?"
2. "He's thick as a plank."

COMMENT Just to confuse things, you can also be "thick with" a person, meaning in a mood with them because they have upset you e.g. "Don't you be getting thick with me."

Yoke *Noun*

MEANING Thing / Thingamajig

SENTENCE

1. "What's that yoke?"
2. "Where did I put the yoke?"

COMMENT

1. Very commonly used, especially when we can't think of a word.
2. "Yokes:" also a slang term for the illegal drug, Ecstasy.

The Uniquely Irish Use of "Grand"

No one uses the word "grand" quite like the Irish. It's as if we've taken the word and made it our own. It means so many things depending on where, when and how we use it.

How're You Doing?

If you ask us how we're doing and we tell you we're "Grand," we're just doing okay, no better. In fact, we're probably worse than that, just trying to be positive.

However, if we tell you we're, "Grand out" or "Grand, altogether," then we're feeling much better. We're good. We might even be great. It's all in our tone.

Still with me?

The Weather

If, commenting on the weather, we say something like, "Grand day, thank God," this is positive. The tone and, crucially, the "Thank God," give it away. Having said that, we rarely have good weather. So a good day for us would probably be a terrible day for most but we'll be happy with it because it's not raining right at that moment.

In Reply To An Offer

If you make us an offer and we tell you that we're, "Grand," we're, very gently, saying no. We don't like letting people down. So we'll say something like, "Ah, you're grand."

In Reply To An Apology

If you apologise to us and we say, "It's grand," or "You're grand," then apology accepted. Don't give it another thought.

If Something's Impressive

If something's impressive, say a magnificent building, we won't use "grand," to describe it, as the British might. To us, grand generally means ordinary.

ASK US TO DO SOMETHING UNREASONABLE ...

Ask us to do something we've no intention of doing and expect to be met with a heady mix of sarcasm and slang:

- I will, yeah.
- I will in me hat.
- I will in me eye.
- I will in me bollix.
- I will in me hole.
- Ask me hole.
- Ask me arse.
- I will in me arse.
- I will in me shite.
- Yeah, no.

Better to just not ask.

A Few Auld Insults while we're At It

In Ireland, if you want to insult someone you have no shortage of options. The terms with stars can also be used affectionately, especially if you lead in with: "you big" or "you auld." Most of these are slang.

Amadán
Fool (Irish language word)
PRONOUNCED om-a-DAWN

Balooba*
Idiot (Often used affectionately e.g. "You great big balooba.") Very similar to eejit.

Bogger
Rural person (Used by Dubliners)

Bowsie*
Good-for-nothing, boozer. When used affection-
ately, it means a messer or joker.
PRONOUNCED BOUGH-zee

Chancer*
Trickster

Creature
Lowlife

Culchie
Rural person (Used by Dubliners)

Cute hoor*
As an insult: someone sneaky. As a compliment:
someone who gets around the rules.

Dope*

Idiot

Dry shite

Bore. Lacking humour.

Eejit*

Idiot

COMMENT

1. Very commonly used.
2. Often preceded by "You big…" or "You fecking…"
3. We often refer to ourselves as eejits: "I'm a feckin' eejit." "I'm such an eejit".

Fecker*

Milder than Fucker (We use both.)

Flute

Idiot

Gimp
Idiot

Gobshite / Gobdaw
Idiot

Gombeen
Idiot

Gowl
Fool (Limerick expression)

Gurrier
Thug

Head-the-ball*
1. Idiot. Head case.
2. Sometimes we'll use "Head-the-ball" if we just can't think of someone's name. e.g. "You know, head-the-ball."

Jackeen
Person from Dublin. (Used by people outside Dublin)

Knacker
Scumbag

Langer
1. Dickhead (literally)
2. Cork expression

Muck Savage
Uncouth rural person

Muppet*
Idiot

Sap
Wimp

Scanger
Petty criminal

Scrubber

Common, uncouth, foul-mouthed.

Scumbag

Lowlife

Skank

Trashy person

Slag

Promiscuous woman

Sleeveen

Sly, sneaky person

Spanner

Fool

Tight bastard

Mean with money / Stingy

COMMENT One of the worst things you could be in Ireland.

AH I'M NOT THAT BAD LIKE

Tool
Idiot

Toe-rag
Lowlife

Trollop*
Promiscuous woman. Often used affectionately to mean "flirt."

Wagon*
Used in the same way as you might call someone a "Cow."

Waster / Waste of space
Good for nothing. Useless.

Apart from Amadán, you could precede any of the above with "Poxy", "Manky" or "Fecking" (Yes, even "fecker" i.e. "You fecking fecker.") for maximum effect. Manky means filthy.

we Might Occasionally Compliment You

If you're *very* lucky we might call you:

A dote
A sweetie (e.g. "You're a dote.") Commonly used.
You couldn't get nicer than a dote.

A man / woman after me own heart
A man / woman I'm very fond of

Pet
Sweetheart

Massive
Great e.g. "You're massive."

Deadly
Fantastic e.g. "You're deadly."

Sound / Sound as a pound
A good guy e.g. "He's sound." Or even better: "He's sound as a pound."

A Good Skin
Decent guy

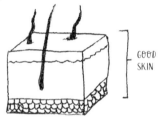

GOOD
SKIN

A Legend
Out on your own

A mad yoke / Mad / Great craic
You're up for anything / great fun. (The ultimate compliment.)

"Hurling" And Other Confusing Irish Nouns

Banshee
Mythical female spirit who heralds the death of
a family member by wailing. Key word: mythical.

Bazzer
A tight haircut. (Cork expression)

Fry / Full Irish Breakfast
A fry or a full Irish breakfast includes fried bacon
("rashers"), sausages, black pudding (slices of a
type of sausage made from pork blood, fat and
cereal – better than it sounds), fried egg, fried
or grilled tomatoes, fried mushrooms. Served

with toast and tea / coffee and sometimes fried potatoes.

Hot Press
Airing cupboard

Hurling
Hurling is one of our two national sports. It has nothing to do with throwing up. We don't do that competitively. Hurling is one of the fastest field sports in the world. Helmets and facemasks must be worn as it is *intense*.

Gaelic Football
Our other national sport is Gaelic Football, also incredibly fast, involving a round ball (a bit smaller than a soccer ball) that is both kicked and carried. When carried, it must be bounced.

Jacks (The)
Loo, toilet. (Slang)

Guards / Gardai

The police (derived from the Irish Garda Síochána, Meaning: "Guardians of the Peace.")

Gob

Mouth.

Leprechaun

Tiny, mythical, bearded fairy who gets up to high-jinks. He'll grant you three wishes if you catch him so that you'll let him go. Though *mythical*, leprechauns are a protected species under EU law!

Lock-in

Illegal after-hours drinking in a closed pub

Naggin

200ml bottle of spirits, easily concealed by underage drinkers.

Rashers
Slices of bacon fried or grilled.

Rubber
Eraser. In Ireland, "Can I borrow your rubber?" is an innocuous request.

Shebeen
Illicit bar where alcohol is sold illegally.

Sliced pan
Sliced bread

Togs
Swimsuit

Trad Session
A session of traditional Irish music, often in a pub. Recommended.

Why Say "It's Raining" When You Can Say...

Like the Eskimos with snow, we have many ways to say it's raining:

Heavy Rain

It's:

- Bucketing
- Lashing
- Milling
- Pelting
- Pissing
- Pouring
- Raining cats and dogs
- Teeming

(Add "rain", "down" or "out of the heavens" to any of the above for max effect.)

Light Rain

It's:

- Drizzling
- Spitting

What We Call Our Mothers

What we call our mothers varies:

* Ma
* Mam
* Mammy
* Mum
* Mummy
* Mother

Our Many Words For "Drunk"

Why say you're drunk when you can say you're...

- Baloobas
- Bollixed
- Fluthered
- Gee-eyed
- Gone
- Half-cut
- Hammered
- Hanging
- In bits
- In pieces
- Langered
  (Cork expression)

- Legless
- Locked
- Mouldy
- Off me head /
  Off me face
- Ossified
- Out of me tree
- Paralytic
- Pickled
- Pissed
- Pissed as a coot
- Plastered

- Polluted
- Rotten
- Scuttered
- Shit-faced
- Smashed
- Steaming

- Stocious
  (Pronounced: STO-shus)
- Three sheets to the wind
- Tipsy
- Twisted
- Wasted

IN CASE YOU WERE IN ANY DOUBT: all are slang.

HOW NOT TO WIN FRIENDS

Around Irish people, it's not a good idea to be:

- Too arrogant
- Too serious
- Too driven
- Tight (mean)
- That *person* who never stands their round

Irish Obsessions

The weather

The weather is usually bad but we live in hope. We talk about it constantly. Like Forrest Gump's box of chocolates, we never know what we're going to get. In Ireland, the forecast is just a rough guideline. On any one day, we could get sun, wind, rain, cloud – and we usually do. Organising anything outdoors is a gamble. We usually go ahead, regardless. Do we arm ourselves in the event of a deluge? No. Irish umbrellas are either lost, forgotten or banjaxed. In any case, we don't like to fuss too much.

Keeping doors closed

We feel on edge if the door of a room has been left open. We can't relax until it has been closed. Why this obsession? Are our homes colder? Usually. Are they draughtier? Probably. Maybe there's something more. Most of us grew up being asked, "Were you born in a field?" if we did the unthinkable and left a door open. Now we pass this concern to the next generation – and they to the next.

Owning Property

Many nationalities will happily live as tenants all their lives. We Irish hunger to own property. Personally, I think it's a historical issue. In the 1600s, our then ruler, England, introduced a series of laws (Penal Laws) designed to disempower Irish Catholics (the majority of the population). One of the many things they outlawed was owning land. (Others included having a trade, practising our religion, teaching our children etc.) So we ended up as tenants on tiny patches of land, growing the most nutritious food we could under the circumstances (potatoes) to survive. When potato blight hit in 1845, we had no other food source. So we starved, emigrated or died in our millions. I believe that our innate drive to own property goes right back to those days. There is an unspoken fear that if we don't own our property, we don't control our lives and anything could happen.

Tea

We are obsessed with tea, our nation's great comforter. If someone is upset, we "put on the kettle." The news is bad? We "wet the tea". Someone drops by unannounced – or, actually, announced? Tea. We're too cold? Tea. Too bored? Tea. The regular kind of tea. Breakfast tea. It's your only man.

The immersion

The immersion is a switch that heats up the water in a home. "Did you turn off the immersion?" is a regular question in Irish homes. Heaven forbid that we would end up with a drop too much hot water and have to pay for it.

Irish Names And How To Pronounce Them

Irish names are some of the trickiest to pronounce. Fret not, help is at hand:

Girls' Names

Aideen
PRONOUNCED AA-deen
MEANING Little fire

Ailbhe
PRONOUNCED AL-va
MEANING White

Aileen

PRONOUNCED AA-leen

MEANING Shining light

Ailish

PRONOUNCED AA-lish

MEANING Noble

Áine (Irish for Ann)

PRONOUNCED AWN-ye

MEANING Splendour

Aislinn / Ashling / Aisling

PRONOUNCED ASH-lin / ASH-ling

MEANING Dream

Aoife / Aoibhe (Irish for Eva)

PRONOUNCED EE-fa / EE-va

MEANING Beauty

Aoibhinn / Aoibheann

PRONOUNCED EE-veen

MEANING Radiant beauty

Bébhinn / Beibhinn

PRONOUNCED BEV-in

MEANING Fair lady, melodious lady

Bláthnaid

PRONOUNCED BLAW-nid

MEANING Flower

Bronagh / Brona

PRONOUNCED BROW-na

MEANING Sorrow

Caragh / Cara

PRONOUNCED CA-ra

MEANING Friend

Caoilfhionn / Keelin
PRONOUNCED KEEL-in
MEANING Slender and fair

Caoimhe
PRONOUNCED KWEE-va
MEANING Precious

Caitriona
PRONOUNCED Cat-REE-ona
MEANING Pure

Ciara
PRONOUNCED KEE-ra
MEANING Dark-haired

Cliodhna / Cliona
PRONOUNCED KLEE-uh-ne
MEANING Shapely

Clodagh

PRONOUNCED CLO-da

MEANING Named after a river

Dearbhla / Dervla

PRONOUNCED DURV-la

MEANING Daughter of the poet

Deirdre

PRONOUNCED DEER-dra

MEANING Sorrowful

Eibhlín / Eileen

PRONOUNCED AYE-leen

MEANING Shining, brilliant

Eilish / Eilis

PRONOUNCED ILE-eesh

MEANING Pledged to God

Eimear / Emer
PRONOUNCED EE-mer
MEANING Swift

Eithne (Enya is an Anglicization of Eithne)
PRONOUNCED ETH-ne
MEANING Little fire

Fiona
PRONOUNCED Fee-O-na
MEANING Fair

Fionnula / Fionnuala
PRONOUNCED Finn-U-la
MEANING White shoulders

Gráinne
PRONOUNCED GRAWN-ya
MEANING Corn / grain

Laoise
PRONOUNCED LEE-sha
MEANING Radiant

Maeve / Maebh / Maebhdh
PRONOUNCED Mave
MEANING Cause of great joy

Máire / Maura / Moira (Irish for Mary)
PRONOUNCED MAW-re
MEANING Of the sea

Mairead (Irish for Margaret)
PRONOUNCED Mar-ADE
MEANING Pearl

Máirín / Maureen
PRONOUNCED MAW-reen
MEANING Star of the sea

Muireann

PRONOUNCED MWER-in

MEANING Sea white

Neasa / Nessa

PRONOUNCED NESS-a

MEANING Rough

Niamh

PRONOUNCED NEE-iv

MEANING Bright / Radiant

Nuala

PRONOUNCED NOO-la

MEANING Fair shoulder

Oonagh / Úna

PRONOUNCED OO-na

MEANING Lamb

Orla / Orlaith / Orlagh
PRONOUNCED OAR-la
MEANING Golden princess

Peig / Peigi
PRONOUNCED Peg / Peggy
MEANING Pearl

Realtín
PRONOUNCED Ray-AL-teen
MEANING Little Star

Rioghnach
PRONOUNCED Ree-OH-na
MEANING Queen

Róisín
PRONOUNCED RO-sheen
MEANING Little Rose

Sadhbh

PRONOUNCED Sive

MEANING Sweet

Saoirse

PRONOUNCED SAYR-she

MEANING Freedom

Shauna

PRONOUNCED SHAW-na

MEANING God is gracious

Shannon

PRONOUNCED SHAN-on

MEANING Wise river

Sile / Sheila / Sheelagh

PRONOUNCED SHEE-la

MEANING Pure, musical

Sinéad

PRONOUNCED Shin-ADE

MEANING God is gracious

Siobhán (Irish for Joan)

PRONOUNCED Shiv-AWN

MEANING God's grace

Sorcha (Irish for Sally)

PRONOUNCED SUR-ca

MEANING Bright, radiant

Boys' Names

Aodhán / Aidan
PRONOUNCED Aa-DAWN / AA-dan
MEANING Little fire, fiery one

Barry
PRONOUNCED Barry
MEANING Fair-haired

Brian / Bryan
PRONOUNCED BRY-an
MEANING Strong, noble

Brendan
PRONOUNCED Bren-dan
MEANING Prince

Cathal
PRONOUNCED CA-hal
MEANING Strong in battle

Cian
PRONOUNCED KEE-an
MEANING Ancient, enduring

Ciarán
PRONOUNCED Kee-RAWN
MEANING Little dark one

Colm
PRONOUNCED COLL-um
MEANING Dove

Conan
PRONOUNCED CONE-an
MEANING Little warrior

Conor
PRONOUNCED CON-or
MEANING Lover of hounds

Cormac
PRONOUNCED COR-mac
MEANING Charioteer

Cillian / Killian
PRONOUNCED Kill-EE-an
MEANING War, strife, church

Daithi
PRONOUNCED Da-hee
MEANING Swift

Darragh / Daire / Dara
PRONOUNCED DAH-re
MEANING Fertile

Darren
PRONOUNCED DAH-ren
MEANING Little oak

Deaglán / Declan
PRONOUNCED Dayg-LAWN / Declan
MEANING Man of prayer

Diarmuid
PRONOUNCED DEER-mid
MEANING Without enemy

Donal / Domhnall
PRONOUNCED DOH-nal
MEANING Ruler of the world

Donnacha
PRONOUNCED DONE-e-ka
MEANING Little brown warrior

Eamonn
PRONOUNCED AA-man
MEANING Wealthy protector

Eoin

PRONOUNCED OH-en

MEANING Young, God is gracious

Eoghan / Owen

PRONOUNCED OH-en

MEANING Born of the yew tree

Fergal / Fearghal

PRONOUNCED FUR-gul

MEANING Brave

Feargus / Fergus

PRONOUNCED FUR-gus

MEANING Manly

Finn

PRONOUNCED Fin

MEANING Fair, blonde

Fionn
PRONOUNCED FEEon
MEANING White

Liam
PRONOUNCED LEE-am
MEANING Strong-willed warrior

Lorcan
PRONOUNCED LOR-can
MEANING Silent, fierce

Neil
PRONOUNCED Neel
MEANING Cloud

Niall
PRONOUNCED NYE-al
MEANING Champion, passionate

Odhran / Oran
PRONOUNCED OH-ran
MEANING White light, little pale green one

Oisin
PRONOUNCED Ush-EEN
MEANING Little deer

Oscar
PRONOUNCED Oscar
MEANING Deer lover

Padric / Pádraig / Patrick
PRONOUNCED PAW-ric / PAW-drig
MEANING Nobly born

Peadar / Peadair (Irish for Peter)
PRONOUNCED PAD-er
MEANING Stone, rock

Pól (Irish for Paul)
PRONOUNCED Pole
MEANING Small

Rían
PRONOUNCED REE-an
MEANING Little king

Ronan
PRONOUNCED ROH-nan
MEANING Little seal

Rory / Ruairi
PRONOUNCED ROH-ree / RU-ree
MEANING Red, rusty

Ruadhán
PRONOUNCED Ru-AWN
MEANING Red-haired

Séamus / Séamas (Irish for James)
PRONOUNCED SHAY-mas
MEANING Supplanter

Seán
PRONOUNCED Shawn
MEANING Wise, old, God is gracious

Senan
PRONOUNCED Sen-an
MEANING Little wise person, old

Seosamh (Irish for Joseph)
PRONOUNCED SHOW-suf
MEANING God will multiply

Shane
PRONOUNCED Shane
MEANING Gift from God

Shay

PRONOUNCED Shay

MEANING Hawk

Tadhg

PRONOUNCED TYge

MEANING Poet

Tiernan

PRONOUNCED TEER-nan

MEANING Little lord

TO BE CLEAR: AA (above) rhymes with Hay.

IMPRESS WITH SOME
IRISH LANGUAGE WORDS

If you really want to impress, slip a word from the Irish language into a sentence, as we often do:

As Gaeilge

MEANING In Irish

PRONOUNCED OSS GALE-ga

SENTENCE "How would you say that as Gaeilge?"

Buladh Bos

MEANING Well done. (Direct translation: Clap hands.)

PRONOUNCED BOO-la-bos

SENTENCE "Buladh Bos!" (If someone does something impressive. Or if they do the opposite and you're being sarcastic.)

Ceart go leor

MEANING Alright

PRONOUNCED CART gu lore

SENTENCE "Ceart go leor" is perfect to say on its own if someone asks how you are.

Citeóg

MEANING Left-handed person

PRONOUNCED Kit-O-g

SENTENCE "I see you're a citeóg. Sure, we won't hold that against you."

Leaba

MEANING Bed

PRONOUNCED LA-ba

SENTENCE "I'm off to my leaba."

Fáilte

MEANING Welcome

PRONOUNCED FAWL-te

SENTENCE "Fáilte! Come on in!"

Flaithiúlach

MEANING Generous

PRONOUNCED Flah-HOOL-och

SENTENCE "He's fierce flaithiúlach with the spuds, all the same."

Geansaí

MEANING Pullover

PRONOUNCED GAN-zee

SENTENCE "Have you got your geansaí? It's nippy out."

Go raibh maith agat

MEANING Thank you

PRONOUNCED Gu rev MA ag-UT

COMMENT

1. Even better than, "Go raibh maith agat" is, "Go raibh míle," short for "Thanks a thousand." Trust me, the shortening will impress. It will also be grammatically correct whether you are talking to one person or more than one. Pronounce it as follows: "Gu REV mee-la."

2. The reply to "Go raibh maith agat," is "Ná habair é." Don't mention it. Pronounced NAW HOB-er aa

Go néirí an bothar leat

MEANING Good luck! (Direct translation: may the road rise with you.)

PRONOUNCED Gu nigh-REE on BOW-har LAT

SENTENCE "Gu néirí an bothar leat."

Gúna

MEANING Dress

PRONOUNCED GOON-ah

SENTENCE "Loving the gúna, Úna."

...ín

MEANING Small

PRONOUNCED EEN

COMMENT Adding ín to the end of a word is the same as inserting "small" in front of it e.g. "Padraigín" = little Patrick or actually Patricia

SENTENCE "Isn't that a lovely housín, all the same?"

Mar dhea

MEANING Yeah right. As if.

PRONOUNCED Mar YEAH

SENTENCE "Mar dhea!" is said on its own if you don't believe someone.

Plámás

MEANING Flattery

PRONOUNCED PLAW-MAWS

SENTENCE "Would you stop plámásing me, you auld chancer?"

Seamróg

MEANING Shamrock

PRONOUNCED SHAM-rogue

SENTENCE "Have you got your seamróg for the day that's in it?"

Slán

MEANING Goodbye

PRONOUNCED SLAWN

SENTENCE "Slán, bud."

Slán go fóill

MEANING Bye for now

PRONOUNCED SLAWN gu FOAL

SENTENCE "Slán go fóill."

Slán abhaile

MEANING Safe home

PRONOUNCED SLAWN a-WOLL-ya

SENTENCE "Slán abhaile, now."

Sláinte

MEANING Cheers. Your health

PRONOUNCED SLAW-in-te

SENTENCE "Sláinte, lads!"

Tóg go bog é

MEANING Take it easy

PRONOUNCED Togue gu BUG eh

SENTENCE "Tóg go bog é, there, lads, will ye?"

A Bit Of An Auld Story

Let's try out some of the words and expressions in a story. Refer to the glossary if you're flummoxed!

Brian Murphy is bent over, locking his bicycle to a pole. His brother, Conor, comes up behind him.

"BRIAN!" he shouts.

Brian shoots to his feet. "Conor! You scared the bejayus outta me!"

Conor shoves his hands into his pockets. "Any craic?"

Brian returns to locking his bike. "Divil a bit. My sources tell me you were out on the tear, last night?"

Conor's eyebrows pop up. "No flies on you. Ah, 'twas good craic but I'm a bit mouldy today. I'll have to get a bit of soakage into me." He glances in the window of the café beside them.

"Haven't you the life of Reilly, all the same?" Brian remarks, a little bitterly.

"I might have if I wasn't so skint all the time. Don't suppose I could bum a tenner?"

Brian snorts. "You've some gall."

"What are you on about?"

"You still haven't paid back the twenty I gave you, the other night at the chipper."

"I'm good for it."

"You are in your shite."

Conor glances at a passing cyclist. "The state of yer man."

"Bike's a bit bockety, alright."

"You'd think he'd have more cop on than to ride around on a buckled wheel. The thing's banjaxed."

"Well, it *is* Paddy Delaney."

"Who?"

"Total chancer. It's probably not even his bike."

"Jaysus, if you're going to nick a bike, you'd think you'd at least nab a decent one." Conor looks back at Brian. "How's Mam?"

Brian sighs. "She's had better days."

"Bless. Not easy without Dad," Conor says.

"You could show your face up at the house the odd time," Brian says, accusingly. "I do all the work and she thinks you're a saint."

"I'll call up later."

"You will in your eye."

"I will so and I'll bring her a packet of fags."

"Thought you were skint."

"I am but I'm borrowing a twenty from you, amn't I?"

"You're nothing but a chancer, Con Murphy." Brian sees Conor glancing at his jumper and looks down. He brushes away crumbs.

"You're a holy show. Shouldn't be let out," Conor jokes.

"Hilarious."

"At the biscuits again?" Conor chuckles.

"If you're looking for a twenty I wouldn't be pushing your luck."

"Sure, I'm only codding you." Over Brian's shoulder, Conor spies a woman approaching. "Sketch! Here comes Biddy O'Malley with her notions." Conor turns so that his back is to Biddy in the hope that he'll go unnoticed as she walks by.

"Ah, hiya Biddy," Brian says cheerfully.

Conor glares at him.

"Brian, 'tis yourself!" Biddy stops.

"And Conor," Brian says. "Like a bad penny."

Conor squints venom at Brian then turns, faking surprise. "Biddy! How's she cutting?"

"Grand out. Yourself?"

"Could be worse." Conor looks up at the sky. "At least it's not pissing."

"How's your poor mam?"

"Ah. Sure," Conor replies, pulling his sleeves down over his hands and looking off.

"'Tis hard," Biddy sympathises.

"'Tis," Brian and Conor say together.

"It galls me the bags that uncle of yours made of your dad's eulogy. You'd swear he was the best man at a wedding. A bit of respect-"

"Ah, sure, God loves a trier," Brian says in his defence.

"You're a good man, Brian," Biddy says. "A good man. Well, I better head. The kids won't feed themselves."

"God Bless, Biddy," Brian says and watches her go.

"You're too soft for your own good," Conor tells him. "People run rings around you."

"Don't know what you're on about. Sure, Biddy's a dote."

Conor rolls his eyes. "Come on in here with me for a fry," he says nodding to the café.

"On me, I suppose?"

Conor smiles.

"Who's running rings around who?"

"Ah, you love me, all the same." Conor pushes in the door of the café, sniffs the air, rubs his tummy. "Feel better already."

They nab a table by the window and look out.

"Would you look at the rig-out on that one," Conor says about a passing teenager.

"Aren't you fierce pass-remarkable?" Brian scolds.

"Ah, sure, I'm only shooting the breeze." Conor picks up the menu.

A waitress arrives beside them. "So, what are ye having?"

"I'll have rashers, sausages, pudding, mushrooms and tomatoes," Conor says, reading from the menu.

The waitress raises an eyebrow. "So basically a fry."

"And chips," Conor says.

"I'll have a coffee, thanks," Brian says. "Black."

"Ah, God. Will you not have an auld spud, at least?" Conor asks.

"Coffee and a potato? I don't think so."

"Ah go on, you mad yoke," Conor teases.

Brian hands the menus back to the waitress and smiles.

Conor watches her walk away. "Wagon," he says under his breath.

"What? Give over."

"Talking to me like I was a fecking eejit."

"A fry is two words, Conor. Why did you have to list everything out, like a tool?"

"Didn't want her to leave anything out, now, did I?"

"You big muppet."

Conor gets up. "I'm going for a slash."

"You couldn't have said that any louder?" Brian looks around the café.

Conor ruffles Brian's hair. "Keep your wig on. Don't we all have to pee?"

Brian swats him off.

Conor makes for the toilet.

The waitress arrives with their order, puts the coffee down in front of Brian. "Get that into you."

"Thanks a mill. You know what? I think I'll have an aul' sambo, after all. Ham, maybe."

She smiles and nods, looks towards the bathroom. "That your brother gone to the jacks?"

"'Tis, yeah."

"Scarlet for ya," she jokes.

Brian smiles. "Scarlet for meself!"

They laugh.

"Ah, he's not the worst," Brian says, guiltily.

Conor reappears, rubbing his hands. "Ah, great. Isn't a fry your only man?"

The waitress smiles at Brian, heads away.

Conor sits down, lifts his knife and fork, dives in. "Class." He looks at Brian. "You're a legend."

"Can I have that in writing?"

"God, the jacks were manky."

"Maybe you shouldn't eat that, then."

"Get off the stage. You auld codger."

Brian smiles.

The waitress returns with his sandwich, sets it down.

"Ah, great thanks."

"Don't mench." Then she's gone.

A new song comes on the radio.

"Tunes!" Conor says, mouth full.

"And you're the one saying *I* shouldn't be let out."

The waitress comes back with the bill, looks from one to the other. Brian takes it. She nods like she knew he would, then heads off.

"I'll really have to get my ass in gear," Conor says, verging on guilt but not quite getting there. "Heard of any nixers going?"

"Would an honest day's work kill you?"

"It might." A piece of sausage falls from Conor's fork. "Ah, lads." He pokes another one.

"Aren't you going to pick that up?"

Conor ignores him, looking at the door of the café which has been left open by a new customer.

"Jaysus, was he born in a field?"

"Pick up that piece of sausage."

"I will in me shite."

"You expect that waitress to pick it up for you?"

"'Tis her job, isn't it?"

"Don't push your luck," Brian says, struggling to contain his anger. "Pick up the fecking sausage."

"Alright, alright, keep your hair on." Conor picks up the piece of sausage. Throws it at Brian.

"Don't look a gift horse in the mouth."

"God, you're no craic."

"And you're taking the piss, as per usual. Why do I put up with you?"

"You know it's just a fry."

"And twenty quid."

Conor stands. "You can keep your twenty. A man has his pride."

"Fine."

"I won't be up with the fags, so."

"I'm not the one who'll suffer."

"Ah, but you will. You auld softie. Cause if she suffers you do."

"I can buy the fags for her myself."

"But no one cheers her up like I do. That's the thing."

They both turn, realising the waitress has been standing there.

Brian pats his jacket for his wallet. "Oh right. Right."

"No rush."

"I'm off out," Conor says and steals away.

Brian glances at the closing door, sighs, then goes back to paying the waitress.

"I thought you said he wasn't the worst." She smiles.

"I did, didn't I?"

She looks into his eyes. "You know, I've been told that I'm very good at cheering people up."

Brian brightens. "Oh you have, have you?" he teases.

"Especially mothers. I'm a dab hand at cheering up mothers."

"You want to meet me mam?"

"Well, you might want to go on a date first, to break the ice."

Brian grins. "Is it asking me out you are?"

"Jesus, he's fast."

Brian laughs. "I suppose I should know your name, so? If we're going on a date."

She beams. "It's Clodagh."

"Go 'way! Same as me mam." Brian thinks for a moment. "She's an auld dote. You'd love her."

Clodagh winks. "Sure, she created you, didn't she?"

Glossary

*Words that are in the Irish language.

Amadán* Idiot

Arseways Incorrectly. The wrong way around.
(slang)

As Gaeilge* In Irish

Aul / Auld Old

Away in a hack Everything will be easy

Balooba *Noun* Idiot

Baloobas adverb Crazy (going baloobas), drunk
(getting baloobas) (slang)

Banger Clapped-out car (slang)

Banjaxed Broken beyond repair. Shattered
(referring to a person)

Banshee Mythical female spirit who heralds death by wailing

Bazzer Tight haircut (Cork slang)

Begrudgery Resenting someone their success

Bikkies Cookies (short for biscuits)

Bin Trash can

Blaggard Scoundrel

Bockety Wobbly. Rickety. Unsteady

Bog Toilet (slang)

Bog standard Perfectly ordinary

Bold Naughty

Bollixed Drunk (slang)

Boot Trunk of a car

Bowsie Good-for-nothing, boozer. A messer. (slang)

Bricking it Nervous (slang)

Buladh bos* Well done. Clap hands.

Bum *Verb* Borrow (slang)

Ceart go leor* Alright

Chance Your Arm Try Your Luck

Chancer Trickster

Chips French fries

Chipper Small store selling take out especially French fries and foods in batter

Citeóg* Left-handed person

Clanger Obvious blunder

Codding Messing

Codology The art of bluffing

Come off it I don't believe you

Comeuppance Karma

Cop On Common sense

Craic Fun. News.

Creature Lowlife (slang, insult)

Crisps Potato chips

Cute hoor Someone sneaky (slang, insult)

Culchie A rural person

Dab hand Really proficient at something

Deadly Great (slang)

Delira Delighted

Divil a bit None

Dope Idiot

Dose Illness

Dossing Slacking off work

Dry shite Bore (slang, insult)

Dote Sweetie. Lovely person

Eejit Idiot

Excira Excited

Fags Cigarettes

Feck Expletive (slang)

Fierce *Adjective* Very

Fiver Five euro

Flah Good-looking guy (Cork expression)

Flaithiúlach* Generous

Flute Idiot

Footpath Pavement, sidewalk

Fooster *Verb* Fuss

Fry Full Irish breakfast

Gaa Ireland's national sports of Hurling and Gaelic Football.

Gaff House e.g. "Party in my gaff!" (slang)

Galore Lots

Gallivanting Wandering about having fun

Gammy Not working properly

Gardai* The Guards. Irish police

Gas Funny

Gawking Staring

Geansaí* Pullover. Sweater.

Gee-eyed Drunk

Get off the stage! Get real!

Gimp Idiot

Give out *Verb* Complain, tell off

Give over! Stop!

Gob Mouth

Gobshite / Gobdaw Idiot (slang, insult)

Gombeen Idiot

Good skin Good guy

Gouger Thug, swindler

Gowl Fool (slang, insult)

Grand Okay

Greens Green vegetables.

Gúna* Dress

Gurrier Thug. Troublemaker. (slang, insult)

Half-cut Drunk (slang)

Hames Mess

Hammered Drunk (slang)

Hanging Drunk (slang)

Head-the-ball Idiot. Head case. (slang, insult)

Holy Show An embarrassment

Hoover Vacuum cleaner

Hurling One of the two national sports in Ireland

In bits Shattered. Drunk. In hysterics. (depending on context)

In pieces Shattered. Drunk. (slang)

Jackeen Someone from Dublin

Jacks Toilet

Jammers *Adjective* Packed, crowded

Jammy Lucky

Janey Mac My goodness

Jumper Pullover

Kibosh To decisively end something.

Kip Sleep. Dive. Mess. (slang)

Knacker Scumbag (slang, insult)

Knackered Exhausted (slang)

Lads Guys. Pals. Mates.

Langer Dickhead (slang, insult)

Langered Drunk (slang)

Lash *Noun* Good-looking guy (slang)

Lash *Verb* Rain, drink heavily (go on the lash), try (give it a lash) (slang)

Leaba* Bed

Leg it! Run!

Legless Drunk

Locked Drunk

Lock-in Illegal after-hours drinking in a closed pub

Mad yoke Someone who's up for anything

Manky Filthy

Mar dhea* As if!

Mé Féiner* A selfish, self-obsessed person

Mentaller Mad person (slang, usually a compliment)

Messages Groceries

Messer Good-for-nothing. Joker.

Mineral Soda, fizzy soft drink.

Mitching Missing school. Playing truant.

Mortaller Mortal sin

Morto Mortified

Mot Girlfriend (slang)

Mouldy Drunk. Disgusting. Filthy.

Muppet Idiot

Naggin 200ml bottle of spirits

Nixer Job on the side that you don't declare for tax purposes

Notions Delusions of grandeur

On the long finger Procrastinating

On the pig's back Fantastic

Ossified Drunk

Paralytic Drunk

Pass out Overtake a car. Lose consciousness.

Pass-remarkable Verbally judgmental. Excessively critical.

Pickled Drunk

Pissed Drunk

Plámás* Flattery

Planking it Nervous

Press Cupboard. Closet.

Pudding Black / white pudding (type of sausage made from pork blood, fat, cereal)

Pull *Verb* Kiss. Get lucky (slang)

Pure *Adjective* Typically

Quare Queer. Strange

Rashers Slices of bacon fried or grilled

Rotten Drunk

Rubber Eraser

Ructions Riotous, quarrelsome outbreak

Runners Running shoes. Trainers

Rig-out Outfit

Sambo Sandwich

Sap Wimp (slang, insult)

Scaldy Gone off. Mean. Rough. (slang, insult)

Scanger Petty criminal (slang, insult)

Scarlet Really embarrassed

Scenes Good times (slang)

Scoop Alcoholic drink (slang)

Scratcher Bed (slang)

Scrubber Common, uncouth, foul-mouthed. (slang)

Scumbag Lowlife

Scuttered Drunk

Segotia Pal

Sesh Session

Shagged Exhausted

Shebeen Illicit bar where alcohol is sold illegally.

Shift Kiss passionately, make out (slang)

Shite Shit

Shit-faced Drunk

Shooting the breeze Chatting

Shop Store

Shower Group, bunch. (slang, insult)

Skank Trashy (slang, insult)

Sketch Watch out!

Skinny Malink Really thin person

Skint Broke, out of money

Skip Dumpster

Skiving off Avoiding work

Slag *Verb* Mildly mock. Make fun of.

Slag *Noun* Someone promiscuous (slang)

Sláinte* Cheers, good health

Slash Pee (slang)

Sleeveen Sly, sneaky person

Sliced Pan Sliced bread

Smashed Drunk

Smithereens In tiny pieces

Soakage Food to help with a hangover

Sound *Adjective* Good guy

Spanner Fool (slang)

Spondoolicks Money

Spud Potato

Starkers Naked

Steaming Drunk

Stocious Drunk

Sweets Candy

Take away Take out

Tenner Ten euro

Thick Stupid (slang)

Tight Mean

Toe-rag Lowlife (slang, insult)

Togs Swimsuit

Tool Idiot (slang, insult)

Trad session Session of traditional Irish music

Trollop Promiscuous (affectionately: a flirt)

Twit Idiot

Up to ninety Hectic

Wagon Similar to calling someone a cow (slang, insult)

Wasted Drunk

Waster Good for nothing person

Waste of space Good for nothing person

Wellies Rubber boots

Yarn Story. Lie

Yera Expression at start of sentence meaning
   nothing in particular.

Yoke Thing. Thingamajig

Acknowledgements

This book exists because of my readers. I write novels set in Ireland and keep in touch with interested readers via my Readers Club. It was their love of the Irishisms that I include in my mailings which inspired me to gather these little gems into one place. And so my first thank you goes to my readers for kicking off this adventure. Go raibh maith agaibh, lads!

When I started out, I thought that *The Little Book of Irishisms* would just be a little bit of craic. It has become so much more. My daughter, Aimee, who has been producing quirky little cartoon characters since she could hold a pen, has illustrated the interior. It has been so special and fun to work on this together. Thank you Aims, me old segotia.

Special thanks to the amazingly creative, intuitive and ever-patient Rachel Lawston for designing a cover that I have so much grá (love) for that I can't stop looking at it and finding new things each time. (I LOVE that the birds are giving out! I LOVE that someone is yelling "Leg it!") Rachel didn't just design the cover, though, she made me see something that I really needed to see. Reading the book brought Rachel back to her childhood and reminded her of someone very special, her Nanny Irene. That readers will remember loved ones through this book is so touching to me. It is a gift. Rachel, THANK YOU.

Special thanks goes to Stan Morrison, who has been so invested in this project from the get-go. Thank you, Stan, for all your inspiration, input, dedication and wisdom. You brought the book to a new level. Thanks, also, to William Morrison and the entire Morrison family for the brainstorming! Legends, all.

Huge appreciation and affection to my fabulous crew of advance readers who advised on everything from content, to cover, to title: Luisa Andreou-Jones, Karla Bynum, Diana Coursey Davis, Marca Davies, Melanie Evans, Nancy Frank, Terry Hague, Colleen Malito, Alison Mink, Beverly Morris, Carole Olson and MaryAnn Randall. Don't know what I'd do without ye.

Hugs and thanks to the wonderful Jean Roche for her inspired and fun suggestions. And a great big thank you to Kitty Boyle who made me see – through her plans to gift the book to her Irish cousins in advance of their next get-together – that this collection of words will connect people. That means so much.

To my great pal, Edel Corrigan, who gives notes on everything I write and remains a friend! An auld saint.

Love and thanks to Joe, Aimee and Alex, as always.

ABOUT THE AUTHOR & Illustrator

Aimee Alexander is the pen name of award-winning, internationally bestselling, Irish author, Denise Deegan. Originally from Cork, she lives in Dublin with her family where she regularly dreams of sunshine, never having to cook and her novels being made into movies.

Visit Aimee at:

www.aimeealexander.com

Aimée Concannon is the Leonardo da Vinci of her generation. Artist, poet, raconteur, wit and bon vivant, she can turn her hand to anything and usually does. *Note: this bio was written by her mother.*

Made in the USA
Coppell, TX
20 November 2022